POEMS BY A SINNER LOVE SURROUNDS

Written and Published by

Ken L Brook

April 15, 2022

POEMS BY A SINNER LOVE SURROUNDS

ACKNOWLEDGEMENTS

GODS GRACE MAKES
ALL THINGS POSSIBLE

A special thanks to my Pastor, family and friends, as well as my brothers and sisters in Christ Jesus. They have helped me see that Love is not to be feared, but to cherish.

ABOUT THE AUTHOR

My name still isn't Ken. This is all happening at a speed which I cannot grasp. I am thankful for it. I've known peace, been to war, returned broken and seeking escape. I now know all the bad were just symptoms of a crisis in faith. I am digging old roots up and planting good new ones that run deep and rich.
I thank God for this.

SEE YA AT THE TOP

THE LORDS EYES

See with the Lords' eyes' not yours
Look beyond the dreadful wars
Fret not on empty shelves in stores
Or the trafficked made unwilling into whores

Behold the ones that go out
For in their hearts, they abandon doubt
For change they pray, for good they shout
To danger they go to turn things about

Pray for the ones' that feed the needy
Thank the ones' that give away freely
Uphold those whose hearts are not greedy
They leave good in step we should seek to be thee

Open yourself up to the good things
Beauty and grace that come with no strings
Lovely people with them the good they bring
Pay no mind to the dark and its' stings

LOVING DIRT

I love the smell of dirt after a good rain
Good memories flood back into my tired brain
All of them good and innocent free of pain
Are not the memories connected to smell a wonderful thing

In these times only smiles I find, no hurt
Such a beautiful gift Lord the smell of the dirt
In my heart I know the truth of Gods' word
In these times I think perhaps Gods love smells like dirt

It smells like us and of what we were crafted
Every single thing intricate and carefully grafted
When God made us, he could not have been distracted
Tis woe to think of the ways we've reacted

I can see but a spark of his heavenly plans
He saw us create some amazing things with our hands
Along cometh the deceiver now we can make wastelands
Fear not these terrors, for we are in Gods' hands

FORECAST NOT FROM BROKEN PAST

Do not let past pain reflect thy opinion of God
For he is not the harsh one, break this facade
Depression will pull you down to doubt, give it no nod
For your shepherd is good and loving with staff and mighty rod

If your outlook is dreary and your heart grows weary
You may feel down his eyes cry too when yours become teary
He knows your pain and feels it with you, so be cheery
Never fear drawing close to Him don't become leery

His word is true, and always he can save thee
He will lift you up in comfort as a new baby
To turn to Him, be born again, learn to truly see
Our kind and loving Father, sent the Son to set you free

The past is gone do not let it define you
Look to the one who is Holy and true
Follow Jesus always his life you shall pursue
Accept and be cleansed, then life will bloom anew

LOVE INFINITE

How big is Gods' love for us
It cannot be measured, unable to discuss
It is bigger than the universe, infinite plus
He even sent his own Son our Lord Jesus

It has no end there is no limit
In his Love our God is not timid
It is firmer than rock or any granite
The surest thing known is that it is definite

We cannot grasp the wonders of his Love
Not in all of Heaven, which He sits above
It cannot be measured, for God is Love
Nothing can escape it when push comes to shove

It is all good and it is endless
His love is always, we are not defenseless
It cannot be covered by tremendous
Perhaps only close comes in word limitless

TEARS FOR THE SON

DE MA LE HA BEN

Yahweh, Yahweh, send us not away
For on this day your Son we did slay
You know how easily our hearts' sway
From henceforth in his name, we pray

We know not the power of what we say
Be kind and forgive us Loving Yahweh
Our eyes have been opened to you today
We see now He was truth, life and way

Your commands from now we shall obey
With water and spirit our sins wash away
He is a fortress in us he will stay
Oh, king of kings we Shama past our dying day

Let us Selah on what we have done
Let us Selah that it was your Son
Forgive us Yahweh it can't be undone
We shall pray Yahweh, to thine Holy one

WORDS ON THE HEART

If ye be still to look and listen
On your heart Gods' commands are written
Tis most powerful, joyful, tears will glisten
Listen and obey in this Love become smitten

The Spirit of truth is in you now
Unto the Lord ye shall pray thanks and bow
Tis written so ask ye not how
For wherever you go you should carry this vow

Do not ask how can this be
Just be thankful that you can now see
It will be the light to guide your feet
Out of your mouth come words Holy and sweet

Tis the great gift to carry with you Jesus
He dwells within so that he may lead us
Do not doubt for the Spirit may flee us
Tis given to those whose hearts' believeth

THE DEVILS BARGAIN

Would you trade spiritual victory
For a life in sinful chains
Just give away to truly be free
To sinful betraying past shames

For these gifts may seem good
But they obey an evil master
Today, without knowing many would
Who plants poison seeds of disaster

Give away all your hope
For a bag or two of dope
Empty your heart of love
To be covered in innocents' blood

Sell your beautiful faith
For a cold early grave
Dare not make this trade
For a life full of hate

BEST INTENTIONS

Yesterday I shared my work
Not for glory or praising words
To show our work can be for and about our Savior
Two cast stones, showed a devils' behavior

First, I tried to apologize instead of hide
Then I found a quiet place, there I cried
I prayed for them, so their hearts wouldn't die
I am not able to forgive yet I've not tried

For those words would be a lie and hollow
In my time the Lord I do follow
In word and deed laid low, heart broke
This pill was bitter and hard to swallow

Now I ask your forgiveness
Those who beheld this nasty business
You know me I did not want this
Please forgive me I must ask you this

THE WAY OUT IS IN

To be free from sin
The Lord Jesus dwells within
Out of the evil grip
Belief in He who rose from the crypt

The way out of fear
Is faith in Him
The freedom is so near
To Christ Jesus amen

To cast out doubt
Is to live in His way
His name you shout
To send evils away

The way out of hell
Is to become His truth
Jesus within posts our bail
The way to the Kingdom is in you

THANK YOU

Oh, when I was falling
The Lord did hear me calling
In the midst of all my problems
He still came to solve them

Jesus set his eyes on thee
He came to rescue me
Though I could not see
He knew every need

In every single word he loved me
Even in my mess he set me free
He doesn't see the way I see
He sees every good possibility in me

Lord let me say thank you
For I'd be dead without the truth
Thank the father for me too
Don't let go in my heart I love you

SEEN AND UNSEEN

I started taking walks
So, God and I could talk
I walk the same road
How many times? How heavy the load?

I noticed trash everywhere
It was here it was there
I decided if not me then who
There was a profound lesson too!

I'd picked up trash many times
Each time more hidden from sight
Some I had to dig for
There always seemed to be more

The Lord taught me about the seen
And much more about the unseen
I dug past roots of the obscene
I must also do this in me
If I am to become truly clean

Thank the Lord the one who blesses
Found in cleaning up others' messes
Also, for the hidden message
You always keep me full of guesses

GROWING PAINS AND GAINS

I am growing in all maturity
In it I find peaceful surety
Spiritually I find more purity
I am finding what I could not see

Wisdom is coming in leaping gains
I know things I still can't explain
Still, I know more to me is plain
Everyday lessens my self-doubting shame

Physically my body grows stronger
Every day I can walk longer
I fell my stamina does prolonger
Even my heart takes more to beat harder

Along with this comes physical pain
My ankles' are lightening my feet are ache
None of this hurt is in vain
All discomfort is worth these gains

THE REMEDY FOR SHAME

I've found a thing that blocks my way
I even know its' very name
It goes by narcissism and earthly shame
I know its evil that tries to remain

I will not even speak his name
If I sin, I repent, and accept the blame
The evil tells me I am the bad thing
That I and it are one and the same

Through blessed God a spiritual remedy came
It's in his word we are fearfully and wonderfully made
I know that I am not a disgrace
My heart knows too that I am no mistake

As for now I am in the right place
I move along in step with Gods' pace
He will not let me lose my faith
For I am better than to lose face
Always there is progress to be made
All of this came upon Gods' grace

OPEN AND CLOSED

Which is better
An open hand
Or a closed fist
The open gives, take it
The closed takes, give me

The open is to surrender
The closed is violence
The open hand is peace
A clenched fist is fight

Tis contrary to what we think
To giveth and taketh away
Do not be dismayed
The Lord showed the way

So today give
No matter cost
Your gain
is your loss

To gain money is nothing
To give it is something
To the needy and downtrodden
By the Lord tis not forgotten

THE PRUNING

Father is with me, and he is pruning
Trimming away the parts that were ruining
He is ever so careful in this grooming
The things he does leave me swooning

The fruit I bore was ever so sparse
For the soil of my roots were parched
With the water growth truly starts
Piece by piece he cleanses my heart

My fruit once bitter becomes sweet
It took a long while and such heat
I felt many times on the edge of defeat
I call upon the Lord and see evil retreat

My leaves once brown and hardly seen
Have turned to beautiful evergreen
I feel no longer lost in between
Sin was my sickness, the Lord my vaccine

NOT ABOUT ME

It is not about you
It is about others
Know this too
Help your brothers

Give freely love
As from above
Be of good service
Consider not if they deserve it

Help in the good way
Do this the Spirit say
In this pray
For guidance each day

Show all good kindness
Be free from your blindness
So, I say be still
To follow his will

FRAGILE DO NOT OPEN ALREADY BROKEN

Tis a paradoxical life we live in
Where to end is to truly begin
You must look outward and help them
All the while dig inward confessing all sin

We walk around with stickers saying fragile already broken
You got to rip it off, apply it to your heart
It's addressed to Pandora this box we open
Danger! Contains vipers do not open, we have to

You have to fall apart because we're shattered
Searching always for the pieces laying scattered
Don't dare try to set them back to start
That is the Lords' place, that is His part
His loving hands will mend that broken heart

The good news is the Kingdom of God
For us alone it's impossible to reach
Thank you, God, our advocate is the Spirit itself
If it wasn't this way, we'd all be in hell

You can be blind and still have sight
No difference between day and night
There are things unseen, but know and feel them
You must re-open the scars for the Spirit to heal amen

ONLY YOU

Only you can see the pieces I need
Holes left by sin my very heart pleads
Oh, gracious Lord I pray unto thee
Come fill me up, only you can rescue me

You lift up sinners and purify them
We must pick up our cross and follow him
All the while hallelujah and amens
It will take all you have to give

Impossible for us to you is nothing
You fill our cups and mend all things
With a word you can break every chain
You alone let us abandon all shame

Let us worship you beyond the end of days
With Holys thrice and Heavenly praise
You are higher and wiser in all ways
You see me Lord, you've seen me always

THE PATH TO TAKE

Sin is legion
In every region
It has many names
Numerous faces

Seven are deadly
Pride is chief among them
It is root of evil sin
You cannot do this alone
You need He of Holy throne

Envy not that of others
Be thankful the Lord has you covered
Lust not after anything
Especially strange or multiple sexual sin
It is the opposite of love amen

Greed makes money your God
Along with it you will rot
There is nothing evil won't rob
Sloth is procrastination and catching
Do today it is a gift, lest you find hell fetching

Gluttony see thee escape from reality
It is self-indulgence and temporary
It is slow decay and full of treachery
Wrath is not yours, seek no aggressiveness
The Lord sayeth revenge is his business

Don't make it about you
It is about Him
For all and you too
One is selfless
The other selfish

You must come to know yourself
Weather your faith, love, and hope is in good health
Do not let this become overwhelming
Your guide is Holy Spirit, in you he's dwelling

Jesus is the truth, life and way
You must be true; he'll know deceit where it stays
So do as he did as best you may
He's always there, even when you stray

Seek forgiveness for all bad you do
From him, those sinned against, and returned unto you
Along with guidance do not assume
Only perfection can God give to you
For he is Holy so become Holy too

To do this you must make amends
It is a crucial task in Gods' Holy plans
Do not hasten thy tongue or scream and shout
Evil dwells there and evil spills out

You must capture your wicked thoughts
Cast them out, or in madness you'll rot
You must become mature in all things
Self-discipline is one, resist what sin brings

Do unto others as you'd have done unto you
Give freely good, mercy, and guidance as God gives too
Wisdom will come when you be still and listen
Then the Holy Spirit will lead, and bestow Wisdom

He will deliver you from the dark, into the light
The power of this is immense
He is your friend
You must invite him in
Never reject him
The fires of hell are set with that sin

When the Spirit leads you think it not frightening
Acceptance is key quit fighting
For that power is in you too
To be able to clearly see the truth
All things are possible when God is with you

Some things can be fixed by the physical
All things can be healed in the spiritual
Do not seek an earthly remedy
To a spiritual malady

Drop any act or lies
Pray to God and ye shall arise
These things the Lord does despise
So, seek to be true and wise
Give praise and sing of His glory
Do not reflect on him poorly

He can remove doubt, fears, and shame
He defeated death, together you can do the same
In His book is written your Holy name
So, take courage of heart
Fear not the enemy or he'll tear thee apart
You wear Gods' Holy armor

You can have peace in all good things
In the battle of the mind slay the evil thoughts bring
There is victory in the Lord
And only there, over all evils
You carry his sword

Look away from disturbing things
War, terror, evil and earthly things
Be fearless in faith and love
Bow down to he that is above

Hope cannot be put out
So do not doubt
Answers to questions are in his word
So, look there, not to a foolish herd

Jesus gives hope to the hopeless
Faith to the faithless
And love to the loveless
You must listen and accept this

He is love and bigger than the universe
So, fret not on worldly hurt
Obey his commands, heed every word

When His kingdom you reach
You be welcome to stay

It is incomprehensible and beautiful
So may you be blessed and always dutiful
This you should say
In His name you should pray

Christianity is not a one and done
At times it might not always be fun
Accepting him as Lord and savior
Baptism, by water and spirit is the start of his favor

It is not the finish line
To begin true following this is the time
Crucial wisdom to know it's a relationship
No retirement from God, to sail away on a ship

Wisdom and faith are but a fragment
The relationship let not become stagnant
Be generous with all good
Align your wills as you should

All things are possible through Christ who strengthens thee
You must pray for good not idols or greed
Do all these things to truly be free
With the Spirit to suffer becomes ease
Stand before the Lord may he be pleased
To all questions Christ Jesus is the answer to these

THE ROCK

May the Lord be your Rock
Look around and take stock
All the things the world brought
All of this physical will truly rot

Begin to seek wisdom of God
Each day start in prayer and nod
Let him break down any façade
Jesus is your shepherd trust his rod

He will break down the walls you put up
Piece by piece rebuilding you with love
In this doing he will fill your cup
To hear the Spirit in him put all trust

Replace the physical with the spiritual
Tis not simply done with any ritual
Pick up your cross become indivisible
Store up good in that not physical

HE IS THE

Forgiver
Cup filler
Over spiller
Grace giver
Old root killer
Heart soil tiller

Divine creator
Sin taker
Chain breaker
Bread maker
Non forsaker
Overtaker
Holy Savior
Soul saver
Way maker

Wound mender
Torch tender
Life render
Mind cleanser
Spirit sender
Evil fender
Temptation hinder
Strength lender

Reminder
None kinder
Darkness blinder

Will aligner
Heart signer
Lost finder
Command minder

One to follow

Example

King

Lord Jesus

Almighty God

Holy Spirit

Father above Heaven

GOOD LIFE

I see God in everything
When I hear a voice sing
Lifting birds upon wings
In every gift he brings

He is in the leaves of trees
The very air that we breathe
His love I cannot leave
He will always find me

I am one with the Lord and the Lord is with me
He peels back blinders the world puts on thee
In all good things it's Him I see
Always he's there, He is all around to see

You shouldn't run, you cannot hide
Many years he knows I tried
In that place is where I died
He lifted me up gave me new life

Always progress don't let me regress
All good things he does bless
He know all your sin so confess
Loving you always despite the mess

NOT ABOUT ME

It is not about you
It is about others
Know this too
Help your brothers

Give freely love
As from above
Be of good service
Consider not they deserve it

Help in the good way
Do this the Spirit say
In this pray
For guidance each day

Show all, good kindness
Freed from your blindness
So, say he be still
To hear his will

FEARLESS

Fear is our enemy
It comes as many
It's the sin in thee
You must be free

If the Lord is your God
Do not be afraid
All tremble in his wake
To live is your fate

We were made to be power
Over evil shall we tower
Never turn and cower
Be not a doubter

Love is our warden
Jesus his name Amen
His hand a flaming sword therein
He will kill the father of sin

Where will you stand in the dark
With love, power and true heart
From his loving grace never depart
The war is coming you will take part

LONLINESS

What a curse I find this loneliness
I have no wife, I have no kids
I own the blame, the sin in me has led to this
Perhaps it is my Lord and I making amends

I sought out lust instead of love
In many I found it instead of one
If this be Gods will, let it be done
Thank you, God, a lesson from the Son

As with all remove God and there is sin
When you remove the Lord the evil creeps in
God saved me so that I may begin
He saved me so I may live again

My focus shall not be on the physical
If my God wills it, he'll send that miracle
I am to focus on the Holy and Spiritual
In that relationship I must hold vigil

MADNESS

This is madness
Everywhere there's sadness
The war in my brain
Tries driving me insane

I'm on the brink
Swim or sink
Full of woe
Head to toe

Lord help me
You do see
Don't you?
Won't you?

I need mercy
I need help
I'm all topsy turvy
I feel like hell

So, save my mind
Be so kind
Send your love
From above

TOMORROW

What is tomorrow, it remains unknown
Only today are we shown
Why worry on that which we don't know
Our ally is powerful be faithful and grow

As we hurdle unstoppably forward
Progress we seek as in the word
What cannot be seen or heard
Focus on that and press onward

In the Lord you have what you need
Already in you is this sprouting seed
Water it with hope, love and faith
We don't know if it's our last day

The Lord Jesus is most loving and kind
Any bad thing put out of your mind
You have no fast forward or rewind
You can always pause, find peace of mind

Tis but one gift he gave us
So, forget tomorrow it could be a bust
Focus on now focus on Jesus
He is coming be patient he'll save us

IMAGO DEI

The enemy will lay his traps
Try some this, try some that
It is fact he's just mad
Nothing for you here old scratch

The Bible's just a fairy tale
Trusst me pal there's no hell
Keep on sinning all is well
What's that sound, another sell

Even science knows we're made
In Gods' image Imago Dei
It's just luck some will say
Do not follow that highway

He feeds on weakness
For he is weak
The Lord strengthens us
For he is strength

BE THE MISSION

Pick up your feet
Learn from defeat
We shall not retreat
Say the Lord unto thee

His word gives us mission
For men we go fishing
Full of spiritual ambition
Seek him in every decision

We know from word the small things
Faith without works is dead
Act, gain trust in big things
Have no fear cast off dread

If you're lacking in Spirit
Selah draw near it
Take that leap, just don't sit
You gain favor bit by bit

THE VISION

Scorpions and serpents what are these
Evil demons in them there be
The Lord gave us dominion over thee
The Lord told me; the Lord God showed me

If it's his will I fight these things
I shall feel no bite or fear of stings
No fang or venom on me as I fight and sing
I fear you not you devious beings

I will fight with the power if his breath
I will do His absolute best
Till the heart drops from my chest
When Father calls me home to rest

Praise the Lord almighty
Glory to him that sees
Give us peace in all deeds
Always shall we worship thee

HE IS WITH ME

The Spirit is here
As I draw near
He works in me
He sees all to see

I am yet to fully obey
To both our dismay
This is okay
I shall not be swayed

He is growing
In me it's showing
Some powers flowing
He is all knowing

I pray good gifts
Release from death sticks
Freedom from sinful wit
The Spirit comes and I am his

DEAR DAD

Thank you for adopting me
Even when I cannot see
Endless love you give me
Regardless of the sinful tree

I know I don't deserve it
I've sinned plenty I admit
Your love for me you don't forget
To help you've sent the Spirit

Thank you for saving my life
Not once but, many a time
A mouthy son spewing lies
You Lord did not me despise

If I may ask a thing
Let me serve and joyfully sing
Of all the gifts you bring
To be with you my Holy King

Raise us up
Fill our cups
Our world run amuck
Wash us clean with hyssop

THANK YOU, LORD, MOST KIND

I am barely hanging on
Fingernails torn and gone
Each moment an eon
I get played like a pawn

Thank you, Lord, for your strength
I'd be dead if it was just me
Blessed are those who see
We aren't alone, never will be

So far, I have to go
Instant rage ready to blow
I've laid myself low
Fighting each and every foe

The Lord fills my cup
The Shepherd will rise me up
In you lay all my trust
Holy Spirit take over soon enough

REFLECTION AND INTROSPECTION

What see you as you gaze upon your face
Is it lost and gone, is it disgrace
Is your mind too busy in another place
I hope and pray you see Gods' grace

What's in your Nephesh, are you counted blessed
We know the world, its' terrible mess
If pride is there you will not confess
God made you to be good and fearless

You are never out of the fight
Your strength is his, the Lords' Holy might
Fear not what comes in the night
Seek truth always, wisdom prove you right

You are his child beautiful and wild
May your faith be radical, never mild
Take back that stolen innocent child
With all things love, may your name be filed

You are not alone, have no alienation
God holds with Him your very salvation
Find hope in good, it's never on vacation
May you in Christ, become a new creation

GROWTH WITH HOPE

My relationship with God grows
Inside and outside, it shows
Still, I have a ways to go
Friends aren't made in a day you know

Always am I near him
Sometimes I hear them
Father, Son and Spirit
Bless God always amen

He councils me when I assume
To know his ways, it's too soon
Gentle, a soft breeze a cloud at noon
Seek his guidance, lest ye find doom

I am with the Lord he with me
Opening my eyes to slowly see
Listening when I simply be
My Lord my God forever thee

GENTLE RAIN

How amazing is a gentle rain
Cleans the air, washes stain
Waters dirt when gardens strain
Its' lovely noise eases pain

So, look on the bright side
To focus on the inside
Time will come for the outside
Beauty arrive as a flower dressed bride

Its' smell is one of stirred dirt
Reminding us we're still on earth
A time will come for new rebirth
Until that time we heed his word

Without it nothing can grow
Flowers with their beautiful show
There is no finer set of clothes
The peace in this I pray you know

WALK THE TALK

Whatever hand life has dealt
The Lord is always there to help
No matter what you've thought or felt
You cannot do this by yourself

He will carry you, when you can't walk
He speaks for you, if unable to talk
Faithful always so do not balk
Take his hand admit your faults

You may have done many a bad thing
You yourself are not that bad thing
The devil speaks as an evil being
Only death can the fallen one bring

So, submit and pray for your path
Shown and spoken without his wrath
Once you take him as Lord, with bath
There shall be no turning back

BLESS MY LORD MY GOD

My God how many times did you save me
In a dozen lives I cannot repay thee
All of this and still you love who I be
God thank you for letting me see

In my dying you sent your angels
Taking poison from my blood, life in dangle
Clearing my mind to see spiritual angles
Praise you always past death and mangle

Praise the Lord who gave me life
Raise him up through pain and strife
To hurt you cuts me like a knife
The blessings you give are beautifully rife

My God, I will serve you
Always forever in all I do
Give to the lowly no matter who
Love unto others as you love too

GOD IS HERE

Another day, another night
What he says, again proved right
Seen what may, in plain sight
Praise Yahweh, you ease my plight

A study of John
Planned days long
Came and gone
Later proved in song

Why chose me
It was to be
For me to see
Give all to thee

Praise our Lord
Bless his sword
As a house the boards
In lovely song the chords

POEM OR POET

Is it better to know it word for word
Or to know the one who spoke it
To think a book alone can save you is absurd
You come to know God by talking to his spirit

You'll not be rewarded for mere memorization
Will be the fall of many in all nations
You must come to know the author
You must commune with the Father

When you are trusted with small things
You will be trusted with bigger things
How? The relationship with God by communication
Within this knowledge lies your salvation

So I pray you may speak with God
You must listen to hear him speak
May you find his word never at odds
Ask and he will say you are not weak

A POET AND KNOW IT

I've always been a poet
Long have I known it
My words grew dark a bit
So, the darkness I didn't sow it

Came a message to a man
Part of Fathers' great plan
I was to pick up the pen
It was time to write again

In my words money's not the goal
It is to find that wayward soul
I can turn hearts to God, he made me able
I pray I lead many to his table

Lord let my pen drip of hope
Father, please teach them to cope
I pray the run to you not just lope
Use me God so they do not mope

Thank you, Father, for this gift
Bless, you lifting me from foolishness
Your will be mine let there be no rift
As I praise, I pray to Heaven I will lift

THE RANSOM

On that long ago day
A ransom was paid
The best ever trade
So you might be saved

The Christs' own flesh
For your very Nephesh
To do this is best
You'll suffer and be blessed

You must give all to him
To be born again
A fight you can't win
Without the Spirit within

You will pain for it
You could die for him
A new life to begin
A heaven with no end

THE RISE

On that Friday plus two days
A stone was rolled away
Death could not make Jesus stay
Only he can give life today

Mary was first to see him
Once plagued by seven demons
Blessed are those who receive him
On shoes of peace, she ran to tell them

It was hard to believe it
For they had to see him
In Jerusalem they did wait
For Holy Spirit to guide their fate

A new way, church led by Peter
Today we call it Easter
Knowing this life is sweeter
On Father and Son, it will not teeter

SERVANT SAVIOR

He came for the sinners
He made them winners
For the new beginners
To eat at the lowly dinners

He gave and he gave
As would a very slave
Past what body can take
Always time for those who ache

This reflects his true Spirit
No reason to fear it
He loved, hoped and did submit
Ever onward he had no quit

So, humble he even bowed
Wise enough to flee the crowd
Knew how life can get too loud
Even washed feet, far from proud

So ye should seek him
To be holy within
Freed from sin
To forevers' begin

THE ANGST

I lied! I lied!
Three times I denied
Our Lord has died
Where can we hide

How can this be
Why can't they see
For he was Holy
Betrayed him have we

What of our sin
We are to trust him
We wait in Jerusalem
The Spirit he will send

He will come back
He'll take our sad
To turn it to glad
For the son thank the Dad

A LINE DRAWN

The Lord Christ Jesus came to draw a line
You can't dwell in evils and say your heart is mine
All will stand before me; you shall pay the fine
If you be good and true, my forgiveness is divine

Do not stand and speak against me I say to thee
I am your way to Father you should pray to see
That which you are facing, that which is unseen
You must follow my way, and I will make you Holy

There will be no evil that you cannot face
You will stand, you are my house, this is my grace
I call out to you so listen, in the kingdom Father waits
The time is now, choice yours, you will pick your fate

Truly, truly I tell you do not be afraid
Bravery is not fears' absence, remember how you're made
If you stand with me, I will come to your aid
If you're with the evil one, you will face my blade

THE DUTIFUL ONES

Every day is a fresh heart break
Mind and body full of ache
A battle I cannot forsake
Always shall I give always more to take

We are hopeful sinners sprinkled with doubt
Closer to the past with every shout
Lingering pride won't let you call out
Still wondering what you're all about

Already mourning this lifes' beauty
Walking towards my solemn duty
A soul on fire burning resolutely
I believe in God absolutely

Each day he lifts me up
Always refilling the fateful cup
It is always just enough
A heart turns soft a mind grows tough

LIGHT OF LIFE

What am I to feel
In a world so ill
Thoughts a hamster wheel
Truly hard to be still

I am surely drifting
In poison thoughts sifting
God brings Spiritual lifting
On my own always missing

I need to speak dear Lord
Let me climb aboard
Sins cut away with sword
Grant me thy will oh Lord

Impossible for man alone
To ever see Fathers throne
Sin and failure what I'd known
Yet I see new light shown

So, I will push
To my burning bush
Heart turned to mush
To hear I must shush

DUALITY IN ME

Each day I can find a fresh hell
A past poisoned mind is not well
Every person or place rings an alarm bell
I say I'm fine, a lie and all can tell

Every day I can find beauty that makes me cry
Those in time see me look to most high
Then I find hope it's his and is mine
On these days all is well all is fine

There's still love here gently I'm reminded
Though a sin-stained mind keeps me blinded
Always past sins seek to keep you binded
So familiar, so wrong I know it's misguided

With help from God, I can break these chains
Hope, love, and faith cleanse my brain
Still, I walk casting off my pains
Lord, I need you, I ask do not refrain

ONLYYOU

My God I was lost without you
Earthly comfort, sin as a deluge
Even then you shone through
Only you are absolute and true

Take another drink or pill
Bow down to societies ill
To that sin, I'm just another kill
God shows me love; he lets me be still

All I've learned can be a shock
With you beside me I cannot stop
You give me words to talk the talk
Your strength lets me walk the walk

Always thanks to you my deliverer
Praise to Jesus, the kindest forgiver
I was for hell, but you are bigger
With you in me I shall not shiver

IN HIM AMEN

Are you spinning your wheels
On sinful cheap thrills
The evil one steals
The evil one kills

He will tell you lies
Give you lustful butterflies
With Christ his power dies
Breaking sin, breaking ties

You can always change your track
To get the devils off your back
Nothing does our Lord lack
Bear your cross resist the attack

He is always there for you
He will turn your heart true
There is nothing we cannot do
Follow Jesus be born anew

BEAUTIFUL GRACE

Life is strange with every breath
Full of beauty, full of strife
Walking towards death
Running to real life

We are to give all
Always for the good
Sins will see you fall
As they do, as they should

Thank the Lord there's no deserve
Only grace will lead you home
So, hang upon his every word
He shall lead you to the throne

MIND WARS

Feeling like a misfit
Instant rage won't quit
I need a respite
I need the Holy Spirit

The war in our brains
Comes with little things
The doubt it brings
Is a song not to sing

Father save me from myself
This misery, this sinful cell
Together we can break the spell
The when only time can tell

Praise you Almighty
Treat me kindly
As I hold on tightly
Never Lord spite me

THE STRENGTH THAT BINDS

I dream and think of you all night
In darkest times you are the light
In the fiercest storms you are bright
You my Lord will make things right

You carry me when I lack strength
In you grace you pull me from the brink
You purify my soul with pen and ink
Wonderful and mysterious full of links

Always let me follow you
The only hope I find true
Loving mercy in all you do
Living starts when born anew

REAL POWER

The lightning and thunder
Carry a sense of wonder
Beautiful and terrible
With the Lord all is bearable

Crashing bolts and blowing wind
So, the Lord say tis not the end
Fear not a flattened field
Your faith in Jesus is your shield

He says to us do not be afraid
Let the wind come with powerful rain
When he protects you from harm
You should conquer any alarm

The Lord blesses those in faith
In him you will always be safe
Of worldly things do not cower
Tis the Lord God who has the power

BLESSED MARY

Mother Mary so highly blessed
Even told could you have guessed
What your son did truly possess
He'd give himself to save the rest

I cannot fathom your fierce pain
Innocent son to take our blame
Guiltless one to die in shame
Did you know it was not in vain

Even as he hung on wood
He was doing what he should
A mission finished only he could
Did you know it was for the good

He came again to some surprise
The Lord did say he would rise
Still today some believe the lies
He was man and God to faithful eyes

CAN HARDLY WAIT

I hear in Heaven there is no sex
Thank you, Lord, we've made it a mess
Beauty unthinkable and blissful rest
Where our Spirit's true passed all tests

You know here the people can be cruel
Sold out leaders breaking their own rule
Trading people for money, as if we're tools
Your coming vengeance will prove them a fool

For many years I made a ruin of things
A barbed tongue spat words that sting
With you my nephesh can truly sing
I cannot wait for what this day will bring

It matters not where I lay my head
I'm truly alive, but earthly dead
I find there is nothing here to dread
Following your path my feet do tread

BREADCRUMBS

Lord, you leave many a clue
Pointing us to what is true
In shoes of peace, I follow you
Always learning all things new

I carry the sword of Spirit
I'm sorry so few hear it
Your love for us is dearest
It flows as an open spigot

Thank you, Father, you make it simple
We love you and try loving people
Your word is true and full of symbol
The power of you makes us tremble

Only in you is there rest
We must pass this test
To be your kin, to know best
Thank you, Father, we are blessed

REGRETS REMEDY

Open your heart and eyes
Things that decay you, recognize
That which you despise
Your multitude of lies

'Tis not a task of ease
For your heart it will please
To let go and truly release
The lifting of this fatal disease

Easy enough so it would seem
The enemy will claw and scream
As always this will take a team
Father, Son, and Spirit let redeem

THE TRINITYS INFINITY

We have the gifts faith, love, and hope
Through trials in life, they ebb and flow
Sometimes high and often low
It just seems' that's how it'll go

There is a rock you can lean on
He's always there beyond the eons
The Loving God our Lord the Son
Whatever will come to him you can run

He will pull you from the darkest depths
Softening the heart inside your chest
So just selah, he'll give the rest
The one named Jesus, tis how we're blessed

A LOVE CHOSEN

We are broken this is true
Fear not, God can fix you
Don't hurry to make you new
With the Lord this you'll do

Our God is hope, love, and wind
Although unseen you can feel them
When you surrender, you accept him
Then his Spirit dwells within

This starts as slow burning fire
Together you conquer your desire
Even when it seems most dire
Our Lord does not falter of tire

So now you choose his love
Sent freely from high above
Spiritually you'll learn thereof
He shows what we're made of

SELAH SHABOT SHALOM

I thought Monday would be a test
Up at four to see the good dentist
I was joyfully wrong the whole day blessed
As for the tooth man, me going was best

Back towards home out of my cell
I sent hope and faith through the mail
In some small ways I was of help
Upon reaching home, a nap found me well

I woke to peace and energetic bliss
Even when mowing, I thank God for this
Off on a walk to talk to Lord Jesus
We talked and laughed, I even caught fish

My phone rang bringing news with it
A family in need, be there in a bit
I spoke wisely about self-digging pits
The Lord was with us, our Spirits did lift

A BLESSED TEMPLE

Societies ills set to deceive
Politicians, liars do not believe
Who to trust who will relieve
In your heart Christ Jesus receive

Today is held by the one who lies
He doesn't even try to disguise
With the Lord at your side
There is no need to hide

With the Lord you can take the pain
Faith and love you build will sustain
When those around you fall like rain
Your temple built on him will remain

A HEALTHY FEAR

I find now I do not fear death
I fear my God nothing less
When I think of the life I left
Sometimes it takes my breath

Don't assume I don't want to live
I know I have much more to give
I will thank the Lord that does forgive
I will spread goodness like a sieve

I praise and pray not because I'm perfect
I worship because I am not
The closer to the truth I connect
The closer I grow to God

So, accept the truth always
On the good and the bad days
Glory to the God who saves
May he bless all your days

CHAINS AND TREASURES

We trade oxygen for greed
Fulfilling some sinful need
It steals what we breathe
Woe will fall unto thee

Money can't buy you happiness
It can do nothing for you at your death
So, use it for what is wisest
To help others with it is best

Live a good life even in disaster
Keep your focus on what comes after
Keep yourself humble and serve our master
In God you find true love forever after

ART OF THE FATHER

The beauty of Gods' art is not in color or race
He can paint it on every heart and any face
To think you know better is to seek disgrace
A powerful sin it is to refuse his grace

Love your fellow people become color blind
Together destroy that poison in your mind
In all good things to seek is to find
A heart after God is a heart that is kind

The birds of a feather may flock together
In your own soul you already know better
There will be no color or sex when united forever
Seek this clarity in love not just in fair weather

There is nothing purer than our Gods' love
It can be found all places and comes from above
From a man most humble to a flight full dove
We rise and fall together choose love just because

LIFE LIGHT

Light defeats the darkness in a mans' heart
Together with the Lord you do this part
The steps you take are the very spark
This is how the cleansing fire will start

You must take the leap of faith
It waits on you anytime any day
Leave behind all past mistakes
Prepare to give all it will take

Do not refuse and stay in stagnation
With evils take no fascination
It will test you it is not a vacation
The Lord your God and heaven your nation

PAINS GAIN

Heed the words long written down
The Lord is coming back around
All will bow to the ground
The trumpets of heaven will sound

You need to listen, learn, and look
With Spirit grow beyond the book
Wisdom gained in every cranny and nook
Guided along with the shepherds' hook

This is not a life of ease
Don't just do as you please
Always let God take the lead
Even with nothing, he fulfills every need

Do not assume you know his will
You must accept this divine deal
Through the valleys and over hills
To peaceful rest to finally be still

HOPING BEYOND LAMENT

Christ, I thank the Father for thee
When my heart grows so heavy
I fear it may fall out of me
To be trampled by my own feet

I find you to be the true rock
Each time I sit back and take stock
When there is poison in every thought
As I see what the evil has wrought

I cannot run I cannot hide
So, I simply try to abide
I always fail and don't know why
I will follow you beyond when I die

I must think on your promises
When overwhelmed by life as is
I pray God deliver us from this
You are hope I dwell on its' holiness

FAMILY OF CHURCH

Brothers' I'll need you in a flaming drought
Be it in shadows or be it in doubt
Come help me, come put this fire out
Bring the life-giving water we all talk about

Life will get heavy; it'll see you pulled down
You can't help but cry and feel like a clown
You walk around aimless with a painted-on frown
Never forget the one who wears the crown

If sins pull you under, they need to be broken
No matter the cost so the Lord hath spoken
Tis no easy path to find the Spirit awoken
To reach this place your very soul is torn open

These things will happen, and they are already
Grow your faith, hope, and love stagnant is steady
When the Lord calls you might not be ready
This matters not, for the other path is deadly

ALWAYS SEEKING

I feel full of lament
Soul heavy as cement
Lord, I seek to repent
Will you hear my consent

Help me Lord clear my soul
Its' selfish sins seek to control
You are my reason and goal
Soften my heart my lips burn coal

Nothing can stop me from seeking you
You are the life, way, and true
Come Lord with heavenly crew
Led to the path my sins in review

God and Son, you are my deliverer
Kindest of all a loving forgiver
In you Lord there is no pretender
With me in love, oh great commander

IMMANUEL

Gods' tears fall down as rain
He sees our suffering and pain
It seems we've all gone insane
Forever to God always to reign

We grumble and sin in hateful shouts
Hearts filled with fear and doubts
Life deals joy as well as bouts
Of heartache and strife none are left out

Did he not say I will lift you up
No fear or shame when you drink the cup
Joy beyond all will within erupt
You must stand for him or be tricked as a pup

He did not come to destroy you
You can talk to the Father it's true
He calms the fire like morning dew
To spark a new one as he can do

YOUR SOULS DEATH

Are you heading in the right direction
What does your heart say upon reflection
When evil comes be an insurrection
Become purified by the Holy resurrection

You cannot make it to heaven alone
The Spirit lead Christ, his fathers' own
Bow to the one upon the throne
Only through grace will the kingdom be known

It can be hard and full of strife
You must give up what you call life
It was really death ruled by pride
You are not just along for the ride

With Holy power the Spirit will raise
Pull you out of your self dug grave
Dug of sins and earthly idol praise
The Lord is your shepherd so turn the page

I AM

I am there when a few gather in my name
They lift up and speak on hope, love, fear, and shame
Closer they become assembled one and the same
For I am with them, and I know them by name

The fathers' presence flows through his people
There is no power in a building or steeple
They are my flock, they are my sheeple
Together they blossom and scatter any evil

I've called you brothers and sisters for good
You know me as only the father could
More will be shown with Spirit withstood
A universe of love is what hung on that wood

SECURITY BLANKET

Make the Lord your security blanket
Food will not save you nor a full banquet
Neither can the soft gold of an anklet
Least of all your sword and languet

Only God can save you
Nothing you can say or do
In troubles he is there too
He leads the way to see you through

Drop any sense of foolish pride
For it will leave you dead inside
Do you best on this spiritual ride
Always know he is right beside

Spread hope in all your deeds
As dropping always beautiful seeds
Seek out those who are in need
The Lord knows and it pleases He

VICTORY IN CHRIST

I can tell you the time did fly
Decades passed as I believed the lie
The enemy had me, wanted me to die
Then the Lord saved me I cry I cry

Time with Jesus is more than was past
He leads and purifies to my very last
No doubt or shadows does he cast
The enemy was sand and lost his grasp

This has been the farthest from easy
Pain and loss came with its' grieving
Tears will come each drop strengthening
I am one with the Lord and he with me

THE WAR UNSEEN

It feels like evils volume is a bad dream
It grows and festers everywhere it's seen
Pumped into your house on each screen
That's just the seen, it's worse than it seems

Nations make idols to power and greed
A monster named progress eats what was green
It's enough to trouble all who can see
Yet there is hope in people by the trinity

Shift your mind and heart from earth to heaven
Our father on his throne, as loving as ever
Many fall away just as twelve became eleven
We know how that worked the enemy is clever

It's time and it is already to talk to God
As meek lay down weapons showing pure thought
Unimaginable is the scale good and evil is fought
Will you bow to the liar, or into light be brought

WITH LOVE LITTLE SISTER

I the younger love you little sister
A g=force of nature, more than a twister
A heart kind and loving carries a blister
Kindness for all flows out like Ister

You have a mouth to make a sailor blush
Always to and fro forever in a rush
A heart walled by pain from each crush
Know this little one you're beautiful to us

Like the garden you tenderly grow
There's one inside as you well know
Don't let this life stain your driven snow
Be brave and strong, trust he who runs the show

HOPE BEYOND OUR REASON

Without the Lord you're already dead
Akin to placing gun to head
You'd be better off staying in bed
Be wise choose his love instead

Our path is a tree with a million limbs
Unknowingly chosen on a whim
He will come if you seek him
A Godless life is forever dim

Choose Christ for he chose you
Knowing full well all you do
All you lowly can have this too
Follow the shepherd as his crew

I say this not to give fright
I seek to spark a hope inside
He sees no difference in day or night
He sees your heart and sees it right

NONE GREATER

Thank you, God, for the wisdom you depart
You truly soften the soil of my heart
Knowing your love gives me a jump start
I can see that I too have my part

Distance makes the heart grow fonder
On this I would sit and ponder
With each sin further I'd wander
No longer shall your grace I squander

So, I will gladly bend my knees
Humbly I shall pray to thee
With acts of faith, I abandon my need
I submit my all to the most Holy

THE LIVING BREATH

I've been given a whisper of Spirits' breath
It makes me think and guides my step
Always leading from life to death
I wait in action praying for the best

It is the reason that I can write
The words on page are how I prophesy
He comes in dreams in middle of night
Our God is leading me to the light

I am only a man and am weak
Through the veil I've seen a peek
I know I have what the Lord's given me
So, pray on and follow always to seek

Only God can give these things
A joy and comfort only he brings
Freely he loves us we joyously sing
Almighty God bless you Prince of Peace

THE SON ALL BATTLES WON

All things are to be in faith
The Lord leads keep me safe
When I falter his won't break
The Spirit, Son and Father YAHWEH

It takes fear to be brave
Fearless faithful march to grave
Not alone, even how we behave
It is your love that we are saved

I will take the first steps
We travel peaks and into depths
Your Spirit sends and gives me pep
Courage given even in our missteps

We cannot love the way you do
All along you knew this too
That is why my faith is you
You lead us on, been born anew

SELFLESS

Lord grant me the goal
Of a truly selfless soul
For it too must pass
Only my spirit will last

A cup filled for others
My sisters and brothers
Abandon all earthly greed
Give to all those in need

Only with you can it be done
To be called by you a son
Let us rise above it
We become Holy in Spirit

THE FARM

Today I drove from dark to light
Same road, but it seems faster now
Lightning flashed yet the storm found me not
The Lord kept them at bay for us

I was on my way to the farm
Time passes slower there
It feels like an oasis of peace
Just the wind on my face and soul

The colors seem brighter, and trees laugh
Happy flowers lead the way back home
I grew up here as much as any place
This one knows me, it calls my name

I came to be of service here
To do for those who can no longer
No laziness found just time on a body
I know God here and he blesses all

HAND OF GOD

It seems it is our will to sin
We must kill this, or death is our cup
We do this by seeking, prayer, and every amen
We must find the Lord to lift us up

Alone it is futile to seek the kingdom
The truth is the cup that sets you free
To find the Lord, you must truly seek him
You want proof, look at real history

We do not fight enemies of flesh and blood
Our own flesh works for the enemy
Spirits of evil, the Lords' judgement a flood
We must submit ourselves and the sin in me

SPIRIT TO GOD

His burden is light
The yoke is easy
It is spiritual
This life is fleeting
What is a life of suffering
Compared to suffering for eternity

He is the way to the Father
The path to the kingdom
We stray farther and farther
Lest our faith is in him
You will seek, or not bother
To the Lord all amen

Choose life that is everlasting
Temporary idols all crumble
To the next where you stumble
In your soul always humble
In your prayers and fasting
No doubtful shadows is he casting

THE GATE

Cast away your sins
They rot from within
The Lords sheep seek his name
Truly he will call you this way

His own enter through the gate
They are called to action, and to wait
You will find what you seek
What you seek is your fate

So, to the Lord call truly
No deceit nothing hidden
To think this is easy
Is folly and displeasing

Always go after him
Away from dark and sin
For life to begin again
He will part you out and within

SPIRITUAL STATUTES

Gods' spirit shows you belong to Christ
He makes us loving to all
His presence will fill you
It brings joy in any circumstance
We are to do his will
To be peaceful is to reflect him

Don't give up on a slow learner
We are made patient to lead others to him
Rudeness is what the world is
Kindness shows what we are like
To be bad is a work of the enemy
Being good will spread like a fire

We mustn't be fleeting, but steadfast
To be faithful unlocks doors to the Lord
Cruelty will show the evil in you
Our gentleness kills many sins
Do not just do as you please
Self-control begins a conversation with God

NO FORTRESS

Good news brothers, sisters, friends
In many lives we still cannot understand
The God most high
His love infinite and presence Holy

You can build a fortress around your heart
God almighty will still get through
He can plant a seed in its very midst
He will sprinkle it with life giving water

Its' roots will grow deep
Its' branches wide and high
The roots will bust solid rock
The branches and vine will crawl over top

You will still produce fruit
To any open to the truth
Even those searching in dark
You cannot put out the love of his heart

CHEMICAL CHAINS

Brothers and sisters listen please
Put down that bottle of chemical ease
Each one is a liar and thief
They bring pain and maddening grief

How do I know all this
I lived that life for many a tick
Eyes opened I saw the deceptions
Only the Lord I trusted hallelujah amen

Even in the darkness God was there
Helping me, though to ask I didn't dare
I wasn't worth any of his time
The devil is crafty, I believed the lie

I know these facts for I have life
Countless times I should've died
Through Angels and himself a life un-tied
In my pain was way, truth and life

CHURCH FAMILY ODE

To Don and Carol, I say thank you
All in the church you led me too
To know the Father, I would emulate you
Strengthened by Christ, you helped renew
This poor lost soul invited into
Your words and action I saw and knew

Lazaro needn't even speak, I saw your family
Tight and loving even in calamity
A faith so strong it almost seems fantasy
A family of rocks spiritually and financially

Jonathan Hitt un-faltering gospel sunshine
Through age and loss, a loving heart most kind
Robert and Cindy, your hearts on your sleeve
I pray to God give his wisdom unto thee

The Aldridges' have wisdom even in lifes' tangle
A daughter of beauty, the voice of an Angel
Thoroughman clan though many, you share a heart
One after God may it never part
Seth and family, you pulse with the Spirit
Your tribulations strengthen, Gods' voice hear it

Ms. Woodall and Ken clan seek always Him
To the world opposite, the Lord joined by pen
I too write for the Lord say amen
Our flock grows in numbers and good
So many names, list all yes, I could

PK, Bridgett daughters of God, live love as you should

I pray God blesses us all
Nothing impossible for the restorer of Paul
I speak life over all different or same
I pray life over you in Jesus' Holy name
If I haven't, I'll thank you later
This book is done it's out of paper

www.ingramcontent.com/pod-product-compliance
Lightning Source LLC
Chambersburg PA
CBHW071928120726
48001CB00005B/1912